MW00416349

Two-Faced Doll

Two-Faced Doll

poems by Carli Carrara

ACKNOWLEDGMENTS

Several poems, some under different titles, some in earlier versions, have appeared in the following publications, to whose editors the author is grateful:

The Breath of Parted Lips, Voices from the Robert Frost Place: "My Mother Prays for My Father"
Illuminations: An Anthology of Teachers' Writing, Plymouth Writers Group: "Grotto"
Live Poets' Society: "Body Surfing with My Father"
The MacGuffin: "Playing Sardines"
Mockingbird: "Homage to Emmett Kelly"
Shifts of Vision: An Anthology of Teachers' Writing, Plymouth Writers Group: "And If My Father"
Slugfest, Ltd: "The Newborn Rabbits Behind My Neighbor's Garage"
The Underwood Review: "At Sixteen I Wanted to Be a Saint"

With love and gratitude to my husband and best friend, Rich, who always believed in me; to Barbara Helfgott Hyett, mentor and friend, who knew I was a poet long before I did; to all the members of The Workshop For Publishing Poets in Brookline who encouraged me over the years; to Linda Walsh for her friendship and inspiration and for providing me with a quiet place to work; and to Baron Wormser for suggestions and help with revisions of my manuscript.

for my mother and father

Text copyright © 2013 Carli Carrara
All Rights Reserved

Contents

And If My Father

And if my father hadn't grown up in Hell's Kitchen, the youngest of eight,
    tenaciously shedding his German lineage, his father's belt
on his back, his choir boy's voice pulled out of school to deliver meat for
    the butcher shop, and if he hadn't become a runner, pulling
racks of clothing through the Garment District, and if he hadn't learned
    the trade, running fabric through his fingers, naming the Scottish
mill where it was woven, the laces of Bruges and Ghent, and if he hadn't
    worn that linen suit, that straw hat tilted to the side, and if he
hadn't become a man of means who charmed my mother at a speakeasy,
    and if my mother had been able to marry him in the cathedral
at High Mass with all the right people there instead of in a private
    ceremony in the rectory and if I had been an only child, he might have
come home early after work and stayed sober on the weekends and all our
    Christmases would have been full of warm roast beef, aunts
and uncles, cousins from Brooklyn, the Bronx, Poughkeepsie and they
    would have come for Easter, for Thanksgiving and not stayed away
and I wouldn't have spent those summers in Stockbridge hidden
    in the tall grass watching one Japanese beetle balance on a thistle and
if I hadn't always learned to smile, betraying nothing, I might have
    screamed my heart out clinging to the chain link fence that separated
me from John, Paul, George and Ringo, and I might have marched on
    Boston Common grieving the Vietnam War, chanting in a crowded
bus to Washington, to Selma instead of watching it all unravel on TV.

I

Tea with Grandmother

The doors to the Russian Tea Room
are carved with bears. The doorman
lets us in. *Mind your manners, Miss,*
my grandmother whispers, as she roots
her hat firmly with an amethyst pin.

The waiter escorts us to our table.
While I stand on tiptoe trying to see
if the biscuits are there, he places
a phonebook on a chair and lifts me up.
I wiggle into position as Grandma places

a napkin on my lap. There are white china
cups with curved feet, gold rimmed saucers,
tiny crystal jam jars with miniature spoons,
a silver dish with pats of butter. She shows me
how to pour the cream so there's no drip.

With silver tongs I drop two cubes of sugar
into my tea, watch the bubbles rise. Now
the biscuits, feathery, white. I split
one open, let the steam drift into my face.
I reach for the butter, the jam.

Don't bolt your food. I long to stuff
my mouth, let butter run down, jam stick
to my cheeks but I tear off a small piece
of biscuit, spread it with a teaspoon
of raspberry jam, place it in my mouth.
She wipes my timid chin.

Child beneath the Table

In the dining room, beneath the table,
she sits between mahogany claws.
Her dolls, prim under damask chairs,
balance teacups on their laps.

Walls and floors creak and groan.
Malicious steam forces its way
through radiators, fuels the room
with the mineral smell of heat.

She listens to the too-familiar rise
of her parents' voices, her small body
throbs with their anger whirling
like a blizzard against the French doors.

Later in the hen house,
where the air is always indulgent,
she'll slide her hand under soft bellies
searching for eggs, for heartbeats.

Memories

Is mind like rain, each thought
a drop blending into pond or sea,
a shallow bath for birds? Or is it
like a garden, images budding forth,
roots growing deep with memory?

The soles of my feet recall cool sand,
my shoulders the warmth of sun.
My ears flood with breaking waves,
the muted clatter of shells, plover
searching the shore, conversations
on the wind. I fine-tune them until
the surf becomes background, the calls
of sandpiper, gull, separate yet whole

like the sweet smell of tempera paint
in first grade, the drag of the brush
on fresh, dry paper, black lines forming
walls, a pointed roof, an eyebrow raised
over a white house. In front, red cups
of tulips on almost straight stems.
And in the upper-right-hand corner
a slice of sun, a yellow sun, always a yellow sun,
streaming down like tears.

Body Surfing with My Father

He smells of sweat and sun
as he carries me through the surf
out beyond the breakers.
I know my feet can't touch the bottom.

I lie on his back, lock my arms around
his neck. His muscles flex under me.
Treading water, he waits for the rising crest.
I know his feet don't touch the bottom.

I can see his bald spot, pink and freckled,
the creases over his ears
where his glasses are too tight.
I know his feet can't touch the bottom.

Head down, arms extended,
hands pointing like the prow of a ship,
he kicks his feet, fights to stay on the wave.
I know his feet will touch the bottom.

Water churns around us, my eyes burn from the salt
as we hurl forward in a rush of thundering green.

Spending the Night with My Grandparents in Brooklyn

Grandmother

I sit on her lap
in the blue damask chair.
She rubs my *medulla oblongata.*
I love the way she says it,
the way it feels.

I've been sent here to keep her
company, to keep her from singing
"When Johnny Comes Marching Home Again,"
to keep her voice from breaking as she stares
at the brownstone walls across the alley,
cries for her eldest son, struck by a car
in the middle of the night as he stumbled home
from *The War,* to keep her hands from curling
into fists against her breasts, no room left for me.

Grandfather

Grandma's having a spell, he says,
taking off his sapphire cufflinks,
folding back the sleeves
of his starched shirt. He puts on
her flowered apron, washes
my face, my hands, ties the sash
on my polka-dot dress. He makes
cinnamon toast, eggs over easy,
in her cast-iron skillet.

Two-Faced Doll

Her father's bourbon fuels the weather
in that white-columned house on the corner.
Saturday morning she lies in her bed
alert to the sounds of him coughing
phlegm into the sink, rustling cellophane
as he taps out his first Lucky Strike.

She prays her mother has fixed his grapefruit the right way,
each segment carefully severed from membrane and skin.
She worries that the bacon won't be crisp enough,
the eggs will be too soft. If he bellows,
Do you expect me to eat this? she'll climb on his lap,
kiss him, ask him if he wants to play gin rummy.
She knows he needs a drink.

She climbs the stairs to her two-faced doll,
the one with the blue bonnet, a wooden knob
glued on top of its head. Half a turn
and the smiling face slides behind blond curls,
another turn, a pouting mouth, painted tears
tracking down. All day she'll listen to the pantry door

opening and closing, the shuffling from room to room,
her life turning like a never-ending carousel,
like fruit spoiling, left too long untouched
and the girl with the sound of leaves for a voice
finds refuge in the space between.

The Trout

Midsummer and the stream trickles.
Among the boulders, in a pool caught
by tangled roots of beech and birch,
the trout swims clear across the silted bottom.

In spring, when water sang against clay,
the white rush of snowmelt could have
swept the fish away but it stayed
like a wedge moving into blackness.

Through fall light, snow light, the intimacies of spring,
it marked the limits of its territory. It seemed content
like the families I saw on the way home
from playing kick the can. Families framed

in ruffled organdy. Fathers read newspapers,
listened to Ben Cross and the Bulova Music Hour.
Mothers in printed house dresses hummed
while they washed the dishes. The children,

allowed to play in the living room,
built castles and forts they could leave up
as long as they liked. Every night
they ate in the dining room.

Their lives passed before me in windows
lit like a silver screen. Their houses kept vigil,
eyes open to the night. Here, near Bear Mountain,
the stream murmurs like a distant conversation.

Here, only the fish, circling.
One specimen nourished by chance.

One-Piece Snowsuit

Every morning of childhood
I woke to fear, wore it
like that one-piece snowsuit
I had when I was six,

the one my mother put me in
to protect me from the cold.
It zipped up the front from crotch
to neck, the hood tied under my chin.

The galoshes went on last.
Their metal buckles jingled
when I walked, then froze closed
with snow. It was hard to move

in that suit. Hard to pack snow
into a ball, roll it over and over
the front lawn until clumps of grass held fast
to the whiteness and bare ground

began to show. Soaked with sweat, face numb,
I gathered handfuls of snow, slapped them
hard on the belly and chest of the snowman.
Little balls of ice hung from the tips

of my red woolen mittens. The more I packed,
the larger they grew until they broke off,
embedded in the snowman's neck and cheeks,
small red fibers clinging.

II

Christmas Past

The roast is always stuck
in its own clotted juices on the platter
in front of my father's place
and I always arrange
the perfect landscape on cotton
batting under the tree: a wooden manger

with a hole in the back for light,
a plaster angel hanging from the roof.
Bathed in blue glow, she hovers over
the Holy Family. I place Baby Jesus
in his bed of hay, settle the cattle
near his head to keep him warm.

Joseph and Mary kneel on either side.
Robed and turbaned, the Magi arrive
with boxes of gold, frankincense and myrrh.
The shepherd watches his flock. Candles
sputter at the silver lips of candlesticks
while we wait for my father to decide it's time

to eat. I shake mica snow through
the branches onto the flanks of the horses,
the seats of the black lacquered sleigh.
My mother keeps folding linen napkins into fans.
All afternoon my father staggers back and forth
from parlor to pantry where he keeps his Scotch.

He passes by, steadying himself
on my shoulder, fingers digging
into my flesh—*What a clever little girl I have.*
I wonder which word, which sigh
will set him going like the switch
on the set of Lionel trains I never got.

I pray he'll drink himself to sleep
so we can have our dinner
in peace. I sing "Silent Night"
with Bing Crosby on the radio,
where all is calm and bright.

Playing Sardines

When the air is alive with fireflies
and the Good Humor man
has sold his last Creamsicle
we punch down fists,
One Potato, Two potato,
choose who will be *IT*
in Mary Lou's front yard.

Overgrown junipers and yews
form hollows we crawl into.
One by one we pile into cellar
window wells, nesting back to belly,
smelling of ice cream and summer dirt.

Crouched down in coolness,
we crunch dry leaves. Crickets
pinch our thighs. Somewhere
someone is searching, charging
the summer dusk. The hair
on the nape of my neck rises.
I wait to be found.

Watching My Parents

My mother's in the kitchen ironing shirts.
She's dampened them, tucked in the hems
and sleeves. They look like Chinese egg rolls.

My father's whistling down the stairs.
He sneaks up behind her, circles her waist.
One hand presses her belly, the other, her breast.

I've never seen him touch her like this.
He's kissing the back of her neck,
where her hair is tightly coiled

in a French twist. He's whispering
in her ear. *Animal!* she yells, twists
in his arms until he lets her go. He looks

so handsome—Gene Kelly in a white t-shirt,
pleated slacks and saddle shoes. I wait for her
to turn and kiss him. She gathers up her hair,

secures it with hairpins and combs, reties her apron.
She licks the tip of her finger. I hear the hiss
as she touches the steam iron, runs it over the collar,

the cuffs, saving the body for last. My father has that look
on his face, the one that tells me he's leaving for town.
He'll stop in the gin mill at Hempstead and Main.

I thought the ending was going to be nice, like the movies.

Wisteria

Here's a photo of me all starched and pressed at five.
Behind me the wisteria vine weaves in and out
the chain-link fence. Its purple blossoms hang

like clusters of grapes. Someone must have loved me
very much to dress me in that robin's-egg blue
hand-smocked dress. Someone wouldn't let me touch

my brand new baby sister, "You're dirty," she said.
Someone taught me how to steer my Flexible Flyer
between the pines in the forest by the lake.

Someone must have loved me very much
to curl my straight brown hair. When we went out
to dinner someone always drank too much,

threatened to punch the waiter for flirting
with my mother. We had to leave. Someone
loved the way I drew and signed me up

for classes. Someone wouldn't pay the bill,
"a waste of time and money." My mother baked me
devil's food cake with marshmallow frosting

from scratch. Someone slapped me hard
on the cheek when I caught her in a lie.
Someone took me to the circus, bought me

a tiny turtle with a rose painted on its back.
"It's going to die," my father said. "It always does."
The branches of wisteria weave in and out

each chain-link, their bodies fragrant, delicate,
flesh and metal intertwined. Someone must have
loved me very much, someone must have.

Mumblety-Peg

What does she do when
the big kids down the block spread her
hand in the dirt, hold it there
while they play mumblety-peg,
thrusting the jackknife
between her fingers?
She doesn't cry. She doesn't tell.

Eight years old. Old enough
to sense the coming weekend
darkness, dishes shattered,
the thunder of her father's voice,
her mother weeping in the night.

Sunday mornings she sprawls
across the living room rug
with *Li'l Abner, The Katzenjammer Kids,*
listening to her mother read the Sunday *Times*
out loud, the section on "The Perfect Murder."
Wife poisons husband. Buries him in the bed of iris.
One day she'll watch her mother
drop pills into Father's rye.

Circus Clown

—for Emmett Kelly

Look how he waits in the twilight between acts,
how he works the edges of the crowd,
raising clouds of laughter
with the tips of his oversized shoes,
how he stops now and then
to brush off his hat, adjust his tattered jacket.

The crowd is watching the bareback riders
but I've been coming here for years
and I'm waiting for that blazing circle of white
to appear on the floor next to him.
Startled by its brilliance, he draws in the borders
of darkness with a broom until the light grows
smaller and smaller, closing in on itself.

Now the circle reappears, moves
from one side of the ring to the other
and he pursues it, desperate to coax it back.
He lifts his blackened face to the crowd for help,
his stark white lips a study in perpetual sadness.
He contains the light in a tidy circle, then a dustpan,
slips it into his pocket with his gloved palm.

I invite him into the orbit of my childhood myths,
tell him how much I risk every time I ask my father
for ice cream. He ponders that risk, admits he's just
an act between shows, gives up his place
to the center ring filling with tigers.

Prudential Life

Outside the bar and grill where neon lights shimmered
like party favors I waited for my father on Saturday afternoon.

Just one to whet my whistle, he'd let go my hand.
I'd stand there in my corduroy overalls,

my Buster Browns firmly planted on the curb, looking
left, then right pretending to search for someone.

Across the street people walked in and out
the revolving door of George's Bakery

carrying long white bags of crusty bread, boxes
of meringues, a birthday cake with butter cream roses.

I stood there until the sun dropped behind the tower
of Prudential Life, then squatted against the warm stone.

Beneath my feet, minerals seeped and dripped, solids
morphed under pressure, bending and folding to survive.

My Mother Prays for My Father

At night the muffled tick of rosary beads
passes through her fingers. She prays,
St. Andrew hear my prayers. She pleads,

Protect me from the liquored lightning of his fists. She'd
like to raise Japanese iris, learn the secrets of bees but she stays.
At night, through the muffled tick of rosary beads,

she prays he won't invade her, that he'll fall in front of the 10:19.
She wants to leave this permanent evening, sail the Milky Way.
St. Andrew, do you hear my prayers? She pleads,

*Protect me from the blows—my mouth, my ears bleed
scarlet rain on organdy curtains.* At Sunday Mass she prays.
Through the night, the muffled tick of rosary beads.

She wonders why things turned out wrong. Believes
it was the beaded dresses, bathtub gin. Her lips rephrase,
St. Andrew hear my prayers, she pleads.

She darns his white cotton socks, cleaves
to him, to the smell of Lucky Strikes and rye. *Someday.*
At night the muffled tick of rosary beads,
St. Andrew hear my prayers, she pleads.

III

Sometimes My Mother

She stares into the oncoming headlights
in the mirror of her vanity. Scotch trickles
from the corner of her mouth. Wrapped around
her slender throat, a double string of pearls.

Sometimes she braids my honeyed hair, dresses me
in pinafores, sashes tied in tidy bows. Sometimes
she reads to me, her voice shifting tone and timbre
from Rumplestiltskin to fairy godmother. I never know

if she'll show up drunk after school,
knuckles white from gripping the wheel
as she strains to see the double lines. Sometimes
I walk home to find her on the kitchen floor,
floundering in the stink of burnt meatloaf,

her French twist undone. Like an injured doe,
she paws the linoleum, reaches out to me.
I face her as I edge along the counters, past the oven,
until I reach the dining room door and I push it
away, let it swing shut . . . shu . . . sh . . .

The Best God-Damned Birthday Party in Town

My father's here in the rec room leaning
against the pine paneling. He's waiting for
pin the tail on the donkey to begin.
He's here to make sure my friends
have a good time. He's here to make sure
the scarf is tied on real tight.

Missy Melzer stands in the center,
arm held out in front, the paper tail
of a donkey between her thumb and forefinger.
We spin her around three times, point her
in the right direction. My father taunts her when
she bangs against the wall, *Whasamadder, can't ya see?*

In musical chairs he plants his feet wide
on the black and white tiles. The children laugh
when he blocks their way. They think
he's clowning around when he stumbles
up the stairs. They don't count the trips
to the pantry where he keeps the Scotch.

By four his eyes glaze over like the dry ice
smoldering around the ice cream cake.
Wanna see a magic trick? He shatters
the ice with a hammer, drops
the shards into a glass of water.
Seething white vapors boil over the rim.

There's one chunk left.
My father hands me a quarter.
I press the tail of the coin hard
on its crazed surface until
my thumb becomes numb.
I wait for that eagle to scream.

Paper Dolls

I want to be excused from the dinner table.
I want my parents to let me go to my room
with my new book of movie star paper dolls.
I'll punch out their bodies on serrated lines,
trim the rough edges of flesh, dress them
in evening gowns and swimsuits,
tuxedos and tennis shorts. They'll pose
just for me on their cardboard stands
until their hands break off at the wrists,
their heads hang down on twisted necks.
No one will hear their paper-cut screams.

At the Lake

My father scares me
with stories of dragonflies
stitching up the lips of little girls.
He waits in the water out by the raft
while I practice my strokes,
shouts out corrections,
the number of laps I have left.
Tired, I stand in the shallows near the dock.
That's when they come
whirring round my head.
My father laughs when I scream,
when I try to bat them away. I don't
want to hurt them so I hold my breath
and dive. Through the prism of water,
I watch their silhouettes soften
against the sun and I rise,
hold out my arms to the circling mass.
I let one land on my wrist. Its emerald eyes glow,
its claw-like feet rasp against my skin
and I touch those cellophane wings
in spite of my father.

The Newborn Rabbits behind My Neighbor's Garage

I watch from the leafed-out forsythia as he scrapes away
the droppings under the cages with his boots.

I want to stick my finger through the chicken wire,
touch their soft ears, but he's collecting every newborn

from every cage, throwing them in the shallow grave.
He kicks the dirt over them and walks away.

I dig in the cool earth, pry those bodies loose.
They wriggle blind and hairless. Too many to carry.

I pull out the bottom of my shirt to make a pouch, feel them
moving against my belly. In my mother's kitchen,

I put them on the counter, pull up a stool so I can reach
the faucet. I test the water on the inside of my wrists

the way my mother does when she bathes my sister.
One by one I wash them with Ivory. The biggest one

struggles, the others lie limp. I try to explain to my mother
but she just complains that I've ruined her towels.

They're just rabbits, she says, calls the dog catcher.
He'll put them to sleep. I know what that means.

I had a friend named Patsy. She got an ear infection,
had to go to the hospital. I asked my mother what happened.

My mother cried, tried to explain, said I was too young
to understand. I knew Patsy went to sleep.

Candy Store

Grandpa says, *Everything*
will happen in due course.
It's too long for me to wait, to grow
so I can see over the counter
where the penny candy winks
at me in the bellies of glass jars.
There are colored dots on strips of paper,
peanut butter Mary Janes, licorice
whips and red hots and my favorite,
orange marshmallow circus peanuts.

When I linger over oatmeal,
he tells me not to dawdle, but here
he waits patiently for me to choose.
He lifts me up, points to each jar,
names the candies just to make sure
I don't miss a thing. He stands to the side
as I run back and forth choosing
until the small brown bag is full.
He holds his grey fedora in both hands,
fingers moving round and round
the brim. I don't feel the press of time,
never ask for more.

Every Summer a New Hotel

Every August we go away to the Catskills, the Berkshires.
My father comes up on weekends by train, plays poker

in the club car. The only place he can smoke, he says. I know
he means drink. My sister and I wait for him to gather us

in his arms like the other fathers but it's Mother he wants
after the week in the city, late nights with buyers,

smoky hotel rooms, free liquor, escorts. Maybe that's why
he imagines her seducing the bus boy, the clerk.

He walks down the platform, eyes focused like a searchlight
on my mother's breasts, her chestnut hair falling loose.

That night I hear them arguing. I don't question why
she wakes us up, locks us in an empty room. I hear him pounding

on doors, yelling, *whore, cocksucker.* Hotel guests stand in the hall,
ask what's wrong. Crouched in a closet, I try not to cry, hold

my body close in darkness, unable to move. Did he stroke my hair,
try to calm me, *I'm sorry, wouldn't hurt you,* or did I dream it, lost

in a moonless wind, my only refuge a house of shuffled cards?

At Sixteen, I Wanted to Be a Saint

On the cruel marble floor of St. Agnes Cathedral,
I kneel, arms extended like a cross.
I recite Saint Catherine's Prayer,

Set me on fire with the flames of your love.
Unite your breast, your hands to mine.
Stain me with your Holy Body.

My knees become numb, my back cramps
but the rapture of saints eludes me.
I lean back against the wood pew. Above me,

stained in glass, Saint Agnes, Saint Teresa,
their bodies luminous, veils pale blue like the veins
inside my wrists, like the dress I wore

that summer night when Jay took me dancing
at Jones Beach Pavilion. He held me close,
his palm damp against my ribs. With each turn

his fingers brushed my breast. I could feel him
through the layers of crinoline as his thigh
slipped between my thighs. I wanted to be taken
away from the lights, away from the crowds
to the shadows under the boardwalk
where couples lay in cool stations of air,

where lust rose like spring sap,
like incense smoldering benedictions,
like the voice of the priest singing,

This is My Body.

IV

My Father's Patience

Blood running
from the lamb
on our plates,
my father spearing
a rare piece with his fork,
steering it through
the gravy, the jagged peaks
of mashed potatoes.
He swallows it whole.
The bell of the ice cream truck
clanging, a neighbor's screen door
slamming, voices clamouring,
Creamsicle, toasted almond bar,
my mother shaking
her head for me not to ask.
That Goddamned Good Humor Man! My father
pounding the table, his jaw
twitching, his fists
clenching, unclenching.

Will he hit me
the way he hits
my mother when she says,
But Walter, she's only . . .

Grotto

A girl runs up the steep stone steps
of *Chiesa Santa Maria*. Out of breath,
hands folded like a paper bird,
she approaches the grotto, genuflects,
blesses herself with the sign of the cross.

The faces of stone seem to move
in the candlelight, a holograph
turning from demon to cherub to saint.
Rosaries of crystal, amethyst, plastic hang
from the iron table crowded with candles.

What favor might a girl of nine ask?

When I was nine I wanted to be the ballerina
in my jewelry box. Reflected in the mirror,
feet and legs one strong stem, arms suspended
in a *port du bra*. Mornings, my soft boiled egg stood
sur la pointe in a special cup. My mother cracked
its crown with a silver spoon.

I envied that girl from the shadows,
wished I believed in the rosary again.

Blackout Shades

My father and I burned leaves in the fall
along the granite curbstones,
raked them into neat piles
that glowed hollow at the center.
At the edges, each leaf drew back,
curled before it burst into flame.
I could almost hear them scream.
And still he raked more.

Heat pressed against my face,
my back turned to November wind,
we burned those leaves until the air raid sirens
warned us to go in. Dinner was by candlelight—
liverwurst sandwiches, deviled eggs
on the coffee table. My parents whispered,
German sub in Sheepshead Bay.

Husbands and fathers patrolled the streets,
voices muffled by blackout shades that held fear in.
Contained, it rose like yeast into the attic
where spies might hide behind
a secret door. I had to close my eyes.

Behind my eyelids, fireflies and lightning,
a burning halo of sun, Father O'Malley's
flames of hell, the black and white flames
in the newsreels, roaring, dissolving in air
like the sugar in my cup of Lipton tea.

My Nana

Wheels of fire baptized the air where my Nana lay,
cradled in her mother's arms beneath the rose windows
of Notre Dame, windows named for the Virgin,

Super rosam rosida. Currents of color settled upon her
like a nimbus. Her fingers fashioned clothes and hats
for city ladies. From scraps of velvet, silk and satin,

she sewed quilts, colored shards of cloth to cover
the beds of her children. In the back room of my father's
house she slept a widow's sleep, relieved from thirty years

of forced nights, her husband's belt on her back, the backs
of her sons and daughter. She never told me stories
of my father as a boy, a young man. She must have known

the signs: whiskey bottles in the cupboards, my mother's
swollen cheek covered with makeup. Shame forced him
to avoid the living room where his mother sat.

At dinner his eyes fixed on his plate, forks and knives
silently moving through stalks of asparagus. Ice cubes
in the water glasses held their shape. Mornings,

she listened to the radio in her room, crocheted doilies
for my dresser, antimacassars for the couch. She wore
a flowered house dress, thick cotton stockings rolled

at the knee, white flesh bulging over the knot. On her feet,
men's slippers, rough felt with leather soles. An odor
followed her like a damp washcloth in the bottom of the hamper.

In the afternoon, when the light was right, she sat in front
of the picture window, fashioned beaded flowers with wire.
Countless stems and tendrils taking shape in her hands,

a leaf tapering to its tip. She showed me how to pass the wire weft
back and forth to hold each bead in place. And when I counted wrong
or beads slipped off she let me try again. She never spoke

of Paris, her baptism beneath the stained glass windows.
Over her fingers petals of violet, crimson arched and curved.
Wooden tray on her lap, rays of sun splintering cobalt on her hands.

The Rose Taffeta Dress

When I was thirteen my mother asked the neighbor's son
to take me to the eighth grade dance. At Francine's Finery

for Discerning Women I stood on a stool while they dressed me
in scratchy dotted swiss, brown velveteen, heavy and dark.

I wanted the rose taffeta. I twirled slowly in front of the mirror,
colors running iridescent, lavender to rose with touches of gold.

I didn't care that I had to roll up my stringy brown hair
every night or that my mother would have to sew in dress shields

that stuck to my armpits with a rubbery smell. I was
Doris Day in *Calamity Jane* all gussied up for a ball.

My mother stared at the front of the dress where my breasts
should have been. She thrust her hands inside, puffed out

the bodice with her fists. *Flat-chested, just like her father's sister,*
she said to the sales girl, who sold us a pair of falsies.

When My Grandfather Dies

My mother goes to bed.
It's the day before Thanksgiving.
She tells me to cook the dinner,
You're old enough.

I know how to skin turnips
with the steel peeler, how
to mash potatoes, whisk in
the butter and cream.
The Birds' Eye peas
slide easily from the bag.
The turkey is a problem.

I pause at the paleness
of its plucked body,
the gaping hole waiting
for my hand. I don't want to
touch the slippery liver,
the gizzard, the scrawny neck
with its stacked vertebrae,
white spinal cord dangling.
But the heart, that small heart,
so dark, so resilient, I hold it
in the small cloud of my hand.

On the Train to St. Agnes High

The dim landscape scrolls by like the backdrop
in a silent movie. I'm trying to translate
Caesar's Gallic Wars for Sister Monica Marie,
but the man across from me
keeps nudging my leg with his knee.
I raise my head, he raises his *Herald Tribune.*
I can see his unzipped pants, his fingers
searching the folds of his underwear, his penis,
limp on grey flannel slacks.

The window reflects the smoky interior,
the conductor, the man. Do something,
anything, I think, but I can see it
in the glass, swelling as he strokes it.
I close my eyes until my stop.

That night after dinner I tell my father.
His finger punctuates the air around me,
You wanted it, didn't you. That's why you stayed.

I am learning to slouch in my cashmere sweater,
to keep my voice not too loud, not too soft.
I am learning not to lick pizza from my fingers,
how to keep watch on my gestures,
emanating no heat, no smell.

V

On Mary Lou's Pink Satin Comforter

We brush each other's hair, smooth it back,
mesmerized by the weaving of strands.
Heads cradled in each other's lap, our supple
fingers coaxing, gathering, silk spilling
over shoulders, the frayed ends of braids.
Naked from the waist up, we touch, stroke,
everywhere boundaries blurred as light
through organza, our fingers circling round
and round where our breasts wait,
our nipples, our skin shot through with gold.

The Signs

Friends and neighbors know
the signs. Friday nights the police car,
Saturday mornings, the sheriff,
summons in hand, my mother
in bed with a *sick* headache,
the odor of Ben-Gay filling her room.

After awhile it becomes a rhythm slow
and dreamy, almost a prayer,
and I awake grateful for the days
that yield themselves into my hands:
a jar of fireflies, an ancient oak,
a rope swing over the river.

In my room, a collection
of small glass animals.
I move and sleep
among delicate things.
How careful I must be.

A Good Catholic Girl

In high school I questioned
whether or not there was a God.
The nuns prayed for my soul.

Because of them
I made up a list of sins
to recite on Saturday afternoon.

Bless me Father for I have sinned.

*Last Friday I sneaked a piece
of smoked turkey from the ice box.*

*Sunday during the matinee
I wanted Gene Kelly to hold me
the way he held Cyd Charisse.*

*I wished my little sister had
never been born.*

*I did sinful things at night,
(hand between my legs)
to soothe myself to sleep.*

I no longer believe in God, the Father,
the Holy Roman Catholic Church,
but that little girl in catechism class

still fears she might be missing
something, that at the last minute,
she'll beg that god for forgiveness.

Wonderful Meat

My father brings home meat,
wartime meat from New York City,
wrapped in brown paper, tied with twine.
On my plate, the rarest piece
oozing into my peas, my mashed potatoes.
I try to keep the juice away, move them
into separate piles with my fork
but just when I think
they're far enough away
my mother pours the drippings over.

Eat it, she says. *Eat it,* he says,
eat it all or you'll go to your room
without any supper and I wonder if
I'll starve like the children
at the Saturday matinee, the skinny ones
in the newsreels with raggedy clothes
and nowhere to live in the winter of World War II.

Eat it, she says. It builds blood.
I imagine the blood welling up
in my eight-year-old body,
pouring from the scab on my knee,
the moons of my fingernails,
or sweating blood
like the saints in Sunday school,
holes opening in
the palms of my hands, my side,
blood seeping through my clothes,
in school during penmanship
while I'm writing perfect *o*'s,
blood like the hole
in my father's head
the night he pushed my mother

down the stairs. She hit him
with a poker, had to
call the doctor, the police.
My father just sat
in the cane-backed chair,
towel wrapped around his head,
didn't press charges.

Like Clockwork

Why did my parents marry, why did he push
her down the stairs, why did she stay?

Trapped in the white-columned house
on the corner, she made oatmeal, darned

his white cotton socks. Once in a drunken rage,
he threatened to kill me, his opened hand

drawn back across his shoulder, my mother
planted between us like a shield.

A mother of four, I kept my hands busy
knowing when to sew, when to bake a chocolate cake,

but sometimes the wooden spoon stopped
stirring. Do you know what it's like

to fear what your hands will do? I wanted to
run away, leave my children behind

but I couldn't so I buttoned them up in hand-
made sweaters, tied on their hand-knitted hats.

Afraid I'd hurt them, I'd take them out to walk
the endless circle, left onto Messenger Street,

then Tilden Road, the code of my father's legacy
ticking like clockwork. Someone wants to

wash their mouths out with soap,
squeeze a small arm too hard . . .

Grandfather's Tic Douloureux

The scent of Faberge soap, the black-tipped bristles
on his shaving brush, the lather rising as he swirled
it round and round in the mug, me kneeling
on the hamper next to the sink, watching him
pass the Swedish steel razor lightly over his left cheek,
then his right, gently daubing his upper lip. He knew
that even a kiss might trigger the spasms of tic douloureux.

It began like tendrils of smoke in the distance,
a dark suggestion moving through
the landscape of his jaw. I could see the pain
seize the corner of his mouth, drawing it back
toward his ear like a shrill scream.

But there was no sound, just the silence of a man,
hand pressed to his face, waiting for it
to pass like a train in the night,
the pitch of the whistle slowly descending,
flesh and light ignited by the spell of touch.

My Mother Darns My Father's Socks

She pulls one inside out.
smoothes it across her knee,
slides the darning egg
up through the ribbing.
Stretching the toe taut
she darns the hole
with stitches finer than my hair.
The ends of her fingers bleed.

Time settles around her
like a thunderhead, collects
in the floor-length drapes,
the patterns of full-blown roses
repeating, roses and thorns.

Where My Father's Heart Stopped

Because he died alone
in a rented room, the police
take him to the morgue, seal
his Longine watch, his wallet,
his collection of dimes in a plastic bag
labeled *name, date, contents.* A detective
drives me through New York streets
to a shadowed doorway, tarnished mailboxes,
names blurred from sun and rain.

The door to my father's room
is marked with yellow crime tape,
his room a clutter of cardboard boxes
stuffed with food-stained menus,
his favorite dishes circled in ink,
Playboy magazines, bills for the rented TV,
receipts from Beth Israel for chemo.

Havana cigar smoke hangs in the air.
His custom suits stand still in their filmy
dry cleaner wraps. Oval boxes bound
with leather straps hold his fedoras,
his Panama hats that always matched
the suit, the season. On the edge
of the rust-stained sink, his Gillette razor,
his false teeth. A Murphy bed open
where his heart stopped.
The cleaning lady found him.

When I was eight he taught me how
to bait a hook, how to hold the barbs between
my thumb and finger so they wouldn't
pierce my skin. He showed me how
to squeeze the worm until its anus opened,
slipped easily over the sharp point,
half its soft body gathering steel around the curve,
the rest writhing to work itself free.

About the Poet

Carli Carrara was born in Far Rockaway, New York in 1938. She received her BA in psychology from Northeastern University. After completing her Masters in Special Education from Boston College she became a teacher of children with special needs, eventually developing her own curriculum incorporating poetry, science and the visual arts.

In 1994, while teaching at Rhode Island College, she received the Presidential Award for Excellence in Teaching Science and Mathematics. When she retired, she enrolled in the Vermont College Low Residency program where she received her MFA in Poetry.

Carli's poems have been published in many literary magazines, including *The Breath of Parted Lips: Voices from the Robert Frost Place, Alehouse Press, Onion River Review, Phoebe* and *The MacGuffin.*

She teaches Tai Chi in Norton where she lives with her husband, Rich.

Note from Author: For a limited time, get a bonus poem from my next book on Marriage by visiting www.CarliCarrara.com/contact and typing "Marriage" in the "subject" area. Make sure to fill out your name and email, too!

34342795R00040

Made in the USA
Lexington, KY
02 August 2014